CW01512504

Original title:

Quiet Echoes Amid the Unicorn Rail

Author: Kaido Väinamäe

ISBN HARDBACK: 978-1-80559-455-0

ISBN PAPERBACK: 978-1-80559-954-8

The Dimmed Light of Forgotten Journeys

In shadows where the memories dwell,
Faded whispers of a time to tell.
Footsteps echo on the ancient stone,
Yet only silence feels like home.

A lantern flickers, dimming with age,
Pages turn in a worn-out sage.
Each journey taken, a tale of old,
Now lost in dreams, forgotten and cold.

Paths once bright, now cloaked in night,
Lost in the depths, out of our sight.
Stars that guided through trials and fears,
Now just shadows, drowning in tears.

But in the dark, glimmers remain,
A spark of hope within the pain.
For every step that led us astray,
Holds a lesson, come what may.

So gather the shards, let stories ignite,
In the dimmed light, seek what feels right.
Forgotten journeys, let them unfold,
As new paths shine, in memories bold.

A Canvas of Light in Somnolent Forests

In the whispering woods where shadows play,
Sunbeams dance on leaves, weaving their lay.
Moss carpets the ground, soft and profound,
While silence breathes life in this hallowed surround.

Gentle winds carry the tales of the trees,
Rustling the branches, a soft, sweet breeze.
Colors blend softly, one stroke at a time,
Painting the air with nature's own rhyme.

Deer thread through the shadows, graceful and shy,
Momentary pauses to gaze at the sky.
A canvas alive, where day meets the night,
In the arms of the forest, cradled in light.

Twilight's Caress Through Memory's Veil

In twilight's embrace, where whispers reside,
Flickers of memory, dreams softly glide.
Stars wane and gather, a dance in the dark,
Painting the shadows, igniting a spark.

Time folds and bends, a delicate thread,
Weaving through moments, both lost and widespread.
Each heartbeat a story, once vibrant and bright,
Now soft in the twilight, cloaked out of sight.

Ghosts of laughter linger, like echoes of song,
Reminders that sorrow and joy don't stay long.
Through memory's veil, we find what we seek,
A tapestry woven with vibrant mystique.

The Soft Glow of Timeless Fables

Under the moon's watch, where secrets unfold,
Timeless fables whisper, tales yet untold.
With every soft glow, a story ignites,
Subtle and sweet as the soft summer nights.

In the rustling pages, forgotten in dreams,
Legends linger softly, like moonlit beams.
Creatures of magic dance through the night,
While starlight awakens the heart's hidden light.

Chronicles echo in the stillness of time,
A hymn to the past, in rhythm and rhyme.
Through tales that endure, our spirits connect,
In the soft glow of life, we find our reflect.

Enchanted Reflections in a Meadow's Heart

In the meadow's embrace, where wildflowers bloom,
Reflections of laughter dispel all the gloom.
Butterflies flutter, a dance in the breeze,
Painting the air with their colors and ease.

Crickets compose symphonies under the stars,
Echoes of nature, soft melodies from afar.
The heart of the meadow beats steady and slow,
A canvas of life where enchanted winds blow.

In tranquil moments, we find our own peace,
And let our worries fade gently, release.
Amidst the vast beauty, our spirits take flight,
In the meadow's heart, we embrace the light.

Celestial Dreams in the Veil of Dawn

As morning's light begins to rise,
Whispers of dreams dance in the skies.
Stars fade gently with the night,
Awakening the world with their light.

Shadows retreat, the day unfolds,
A canvas brushed with hues of gold.
Nature sings, a soothing song,
Inviting all where they belong.

In the horizon, colors blend,
Every moment a chance to mend.
Celestial hearts, they beat as one,
In the embrace of the dawn begun.

With every breath, a promise made,
In the light, our fears will fade.
Join the dance, the universe spins,
In the dawn, our journey begins.

Flickers of Light in Still Waters

In the stillness where secrets lie,
Flickers of light spark and fly.
Reflections shimmer, tales untold,
Capturing moments, precious gold.

Ripples form with every sigh,
Caressing dreams that drift and die.
In the depths, the silent plea,
Whispers of hope, longing to be free.

Beneath the surface, worlds awake,
Dancing shadows, the silence breaks.
Each flicker glints like fleeting stars,
Mapping our journeys, near and far.

With gentle waves, the night draws near,
Embracing love, cutting through fear.
Still waters hold the light so bright,
A lullaby in the tranquil night.

Unseen Melodies Among Whispering Trees

In tangled branches, secrets hum,
A symphony where hearts succumb.
Leaves rustle softly, a tender caress,
Unseen melodies in nature's dress.

Roots intertwine, stories they share,
Whispering tales of love and care.
In the cool shade, time stands still,
Every sigh, a heart's sweet thrill.

Beneath the boughs, the world slows down,
In nature's arms, we wear no frown.
Echoes linger in the air,
Breathing life with every prayer.

Among the trees, a bond is found,
With each melody, our souls unbound.
In the magic of the whispering breeze,
Dance with the unseen among the trees.

The Lingering Hush of Ancient Woods

In the depths of ancient wood,
Silence speaks where echoes stood.
Mossy paths weave tales of time,
Each step a part of nature's rhyme.

Gnarled branches hold the skies,
Secrets cloaked in leafy lies.
Mist drapes low, a gentle shroud,
Cradling memories in its crowd.

The hush envelops like a friend,
Whispering truths that never end.
Each flicker of light, a legacy,
Woven with threads of mystery.

Ancient woods with stories vast,
Guarding wisdom of the past.
In every corner, shadows play,
The lingering hush will always stay.

Echoes of Luminescent Dreams

In realms where starlight weaves the night,
Whispers dance in gentle flight.
Colors blend in twilight hues,
Shadows flicker, softly muse.

Moonlit streams reflect the skies,
Secrets held in shrouded sighs.
Each thought, a star, begins to gleam,
We wander through a waking dream.

Voices in the ether play,
Guiding us on this mystic way.
Fleeting moments, bright and rare,
Twisting fate with tender care.

The air is thick with stories old,
Quiet mysteries yet untold.
With every step, the past awakes,
In luminescent waves, it breaks.

As dawn approaches, shadows fade,
But echoes linger in cascade.
In the heart, the light endures,
Within our souls, the dream is pure.

The Hush of Twilight's Embrace

In quiet dusk, a calm descends,
Where day and night become old friends.
The sky aflame, a burning fire,
Embracing dreams, igniting desire.

Crickets chirp in low refrain,
A soft reminder of night's domain.
The stars peek out, their lights so bright,
Blanketing the world in soft twilight.

Trees whisper secrets to the breeze,
Sweeping leaves, they flutter with ease.
A lullaby of nature's grace,
In twilight's arms, we find our place.

Moonrise paints the world in glow,
Illuminating paths we know.
Shadows stretch and softly play,
As night enfolds the end of day.

In this stillness, hearts unite,
Finding solace in the night.
The hush of twilight's gentle clasp,
In its serenity, we gasp.

Phantoms of the Dappled Glade

In sunlight's kiss, the shadows weave,
A tapestry that's hard to leave.
Ghostly forms in dappled light,
Whispers float from height to height.

Among the trees, the phantoms glide,
In haunted woods, where dreams reside.
Each rustling leaf, a sigh of lore,
Calling softly from forest floor.

The air is thick with magic's thread,
Tales of those who once had tread.
With every step, the glade reveals,
Ethereal truths that time conceals.

Footfalls echo in the past,
While fleeting glimpses fade so fast.
A glimpse of life, a fleeting dance,
In dappled light, we take our chance.

As evening falls, the shadows grow,
Mysteries in twilight's glow.
The phantoms linger, hearts aglow,
In this enchanted world, we flow.

Threads of Silence in a Starlit Forest

Beneath the stars, the silence sings,
Where nature whispers secret things.
The forest breathes, a tranquil grace,
In shadows deep, we find our place.

Each step we take on mossy ground,
With gentle echoes all around.
The night unfolds its velvet cloak,
In starlit glades, the heart awoke.

Trees stand watch, their branches weave,
A fortress where the mind believes.
In stillness found, the world an art,
Threads of silence weave the heart.

Above, the cosmos twinkle bright,
Guiding us through the canvas night.
In sacred woods, the calm enfolds,
As ancient mysteries unfold.

The path ahead, a silver thread,
In every whisper, hopes are fed.
We journey on through time and space,
In the starlit forest's warm embrace.

Distant Fables in the Still Night

Whispers float on moonlit dreams,
Hidden tales in silvery beams.
The stars weave stories, soft and bright,
Guiding hearts through endless night.

Ancient echoes in the breeze,
Softly singing through the trees.
Lost in wonder, we seek more,
Magic waits at every door.

Time stands still, the world at peace,
In this moment, all doubts cease.
Fables dance in shadowed light,
Revealing truths beyond our sight.

Gentle sighs of night unfold,
Secrets held in silence bold.
In the stillness, we shall roam,
Finding solace, finding home.

So listen close, dear friend of mine,
For distant fables intertwine.
In the quiet, hearts take flight,
Wrapped in warmth, through the still night.

The Embrace of the Nightingale's Song

Underneath the silver glow,
Nightingales in twilight flow.
Their sweet melodies take wing,
In the dark, the heart will sing.

A serenade of love and grace,
Whispers soft in a tender space.
Through the branches, notes cascade,
In their rhythm, dreams are made.

In the garden, shadows sway,
Nightingales sing of love's ballet.
Each flutter, a promise shared,
In the night, no hearts are scared.

With every note, the world ignites,
Painting stars in gentle lights.
Lost in tunes that softly blend,
In their song, we find a friend.

So let us dance, entwined as one,
'Neath the gaze of the gentle sun.
In the embrace of their sweet song,
Together, we shall sing along.

Tides of Tranquility in the Enchanted Wild

Through the woods where whispers dwell,
Nature sings a soothing spell.
Each rustle of leaf, a soft caress,
In this wild, we find our rest.

Moonlit paths and gentle streams,
Softly flowing with our dreams.
In the quiet, we are free,
United with the wild's decree.

Tides of calm, they ebb and flow,
Guiding us where the wild things grow.
Every heartbeat, every sigh,
In this moment, we can fly.

Whispering pines embrace the night,
Stars above lend us their light.
In the enchanted wild, we roam,
Finding here our second home.

So linger long where time stands still,
In the woods, the heart shall fill.
Tides of tranquility arise,
In the wild, beneath the skies.

Threads of Laughter in Lost Woods

Amidst the trees, laughter weaves,
Echoes dance with whispered leaves.
In lost woods, joy takes its flight,
Radiant hearts, a pure delight.

Chasing shadows, footsteps light,
Spinning stories 'til the night.
With each giggle, spirits soar,
In this realm, we crave for more.

Memories twine in whispered breeze,
Sharing secrets, hearts at ease.
With friends around, the world is bright,
Threading laughter through the night.

In the stillness, joy's refrain,
A melody that breaks the chain.
Finding magic in each glance,
In lost woods, our hearts will dance.

So gather close, let's weave anew,
With every laugh, a bond so true.
In the embrace of nature's call,
Together, let our laughter fall.

The Glow of Distant Memories

Whispers echo from the past,
As shadows dance in fading light.
Each moment captured, fading fast,
Yet in my heart, they burn so bright.

Faces smile through silver haze,
Laughter lingers on the breeze.
Time's embrace in warmest rays,
Hold these fragments, if you please.

Rustling leaves remind me well,
Of tales told by fire's gleam.
In the night, a soft-spun spell,
Awakens thoughts in twilight's dream.

Through the mist, I seek a sign,
A guiding star, a gentle hand.
In the quiet, memories shine,
A tapestry of time so grand.

In every heartbeat, echoes call,
The glow of yesterdays untold.
Though shadows rise and moments fall,
Their warmth remains, a touch of gold.

Whirling in a Dreamer's Haven

In fields of thought, I spin and twirl,
Where colors blend and visions play.
Each day transcends, a dance unfurled,
Beneath the veil of soft ballet.

Clouds drift slowly, thoughts unfurl,
As dreams take flight on wings of night.
In whispered wishes, hopes will swirl,
Guided by stars, so pure, so bright.

A world alive with secret sighs,
Where echoes fill the silent air.
In this haven, magic lies,
With every moment, dreams laid bare.

With open heart, I dive within,
To taste the sweetness of the skies.
Through endless bounds, my thoughts spin,
Where every truth is cloaked in lies.

As shadows whisper softly near,
I lose myself in twilight's play.
In this escape, I shed my fear,
And find my peace in night's ballet.

Harmonies from the Mystic Grove

In shadows deep, a melody,
Rings through the air, so pure, so sweet.
The trees sway gently, setting free,
A chorus of life beneath my feet.

With every note, the spirits dance,
In harmony with nature's breath.
Here, lost souls find their second chance,
In whispers soft, they conquer death.

Moonlight casts a spell of grace,
As owl calls from the ancient boughs.
Each echo finds a resting place,
In this grove that timelessly allows.

A symphony of thoughts divine,
With every rustle, every sigh.
In nature's arms, my heart can pine,
For unseen wonders passing by.

This harmony, a tender thread,
That weaves the night with whispered dreams.
Within this grove, our stories spread,
And life's pure magic softly gleams.

Embers of Forgotten Stories

The embers glow in twilight's touch,
As tales unfold in flick'ring light.
Each crackle speaks of time's great clutch,
Holding whispers of the night.

Beneath the ash, memories wait,
Of love, of loss, of joys extreme.
In every spark, a fated fate,
Where dreams alight on midnight's beam.

Let time unravel, weave the thread,
Of lives entwined in dance and fire.
Lost words find life in moments said,
A tapestry of deep desire.

In shadows cast, the stories linger,
Echoes of laughter, tears, and praise.
With every flame, I feel the finger,
Of fate that writes in endless ways.

Together wrapped in whispered lore,
We gather 'round, both young and old.
In embers' glow, we seek for more,
Collecting dreams, our tales retold.

A Glistening Silence in the Forest's Heart

Beneath the boughs, a quiet sigh,
Leaves shimmer softly, where shadows lie.
A brook's gentle murmur, a secret stream,
In the heart of the forest, nature's dream.

Mist weaves through branches, a silken thread,
The hush of the twilight, where footsteps tread.
Stars blink above in the deepening blue,
While whispers of silence cradle the dew.

Moss carpets the path, a lush, green bed,
Where stories of ages feel softly fed.
Breeze carries tales of the trees so tall,
In this sacred silence, I hear their call.

A glistening silence, a treasure so rare,
In the forest's heart, I breathe the air.
Time slips away, like the shadows that play,
In the gentle embrace of the fading day.

Reverberations Among the Mythic Pines

In the stillness, echoes softly cling,
Wind has a tale that the pines will sing.
Ancient voices in a rhythmic dance,
Among the giants, lost in a trance.

Moonlight filters through the needle's shade,
A luminescent world, nature's parade.
Footsteps are whispers, a ghostly tread,
As shadows of giants weave stories ahead.

From the roots to the crowns, a message flows,
In the air, a secret that only one knows.
The heart of the forest beats steady and true,
In the embrace of the pines, I find my view.

A blanket of starlight, woven so wise,
Wrapped in the arms of the night's surprise.
Reverberations, in each rustle and sigh,
A connection with nature that pierces the sky.

Celestial Glimmers in a Dreamer's Haven

In a realm where shadows kiss the light,
Dreamers dance under a blanket bright.
Celestial glimmers weave through the air,
A haven of visions, beyond compare.

Stars spill secrets in the velvet night,
Whispers of dreams taking graceful flight.
A starlit canvas where wishes are made,
Illuminating paths through the thickest shade.

Moonbeams caress the slumbering earth,
In the hush of the dark, a moment's worth.
Crickets serenade the dreamer's muse,
In this sacred space, they never lose.

Colors of night blend with soft silver hues,
Magic awakens in night's gentle blues.
Celestial glimmers, a whispering balm,
In a dreamer's haven, the world is calm.

Twilight's Tapestry of Whispers

As dusk settles in, the day takes a bow,
Twilight spreads secrets upon the brow.
Shadows stretch long in the waning light,
Wrapped in a tapestry woven by night.

Softly, the stars blink awake, one by one,
Painting the sky with the stroke of the sun.
Whispers of creatures just waking from sleep,
In twilight's embrace, mysteries keep.

The colors of evening blend grace and despair,
While nature hums softly, a soothing prayer.
Branches entwined share the tales of the day,
As twilight drapes sorrow in shades of gray.

A symphony cradles each breath of the air,
Where fireflies dance without any care.
In twilight's embrace, we find our way home,
Through whispers of night, where dreamers roam.

The Stillness of the Celestial Dance

Stars whisper softly in the night,
Their gentle glow, a warm delight.
The moon spins slow in velvet skies,
Nature holds its breath, as time flies.

Waves of silence brush the trees,
Echoes carried by cool, soft breeze.
In this tranquil, cosmic ballet,
Dreams take flight and drift away.

Galaxies twirl, like dancers bold,
In a tale of light, long since told.
Each twinkling orb a secret kept,
In this vast realm, where we have leapt.

Stillness wraps the world in grace,
Every heartbeat finds its place.
In the depths of night, we find peace,
As the celestial dance will not cease.

In the quiet, we dare to wish,
For harmony in every dish.
With hearts alight, we join the trance,
Lost in the stillness of the dance.

Ghostly Harmonies in Tender Night

Beneath the stars, shadows creep,
Whispers linger, secrets keep.
Ghostly echoes fill the air,
Softly woven, threads of care.

Moonlit paths invite the brave,
To dance in dreams, the night to save.
With every sigh, old tales arise,
In the tender glow, the spirit flies.

Specters of the past, so near,
Carrying tales for ears to hear.
In the night, they sing a song,
Of love and loss, where hearts belong.

Rippling fog, a chilling sweep,
Promises lost, yet memories seep.
Harmonies drift on the breeze,
In haunting notes, the heart finds ease.

So let the night embrace your soul,
In its depths, you will feel whole.
With whispered truths in shadows bright,
You'll find your peace in tender night.

Secrets of the Moonlit Realm

In the realm where moonlight weaves,
Mysteries dance among the leaves.
Silvery beams cast tender spells,
Filling the night with whispered bells.

Crickets sing their secret song,
In this magic, we all belong.
Every glimmer tells a tale,
Of the soft glow that will not pale.

Hidden paths beneath the trees,
Guide lost souls on the gentle breeze.
In moonlit dreams, the heart can roam,
Finding solace, a place called home.

Wanderers pause in quiet awe,
As nature shows its ancient law.
The night reveals what words can't say,
In secrets kept until the day.

So close your eyes and drift away,
Into the night where shadows play.
Embrace the secrets held above,
In the moonlit realm, you'll find love.

Lullabies from the Ancient Glade

In the glade where the silence sings,
Lullabies weave from nature's strings.
Softly, the trees hum a tune,
As stars awaken, brightening soon.

Cradled in the arms of night,
Dreams take flight on soft moonlight.
The whispers of leaves, a gentle balm,
To soothe the weary and bring calm.

Wisps of fog caress the ground,
In this sacred space, peace is found.
Ancient tales in shadows stir,
Calling the heart to once confer.

Each note of night, a soft embrace,
Wrapped in warmth, a sacred space.
Guardian spirits watch with care,
As lullabies drift through the air.

So let the woods sing sweet and low,
In every breath, the magic flow.
Through ancient glades, the calm remains,
A soothing balm for weary pains.

Whispers of Celestial Trails

Stars shimmer softly above,
Guiding dreams with gentle light.
Winds carry tales of love,
Whispering through the quiet night.

Each twinkle holds a secret,
An echo from a distant place.
Time dances in this moment,
Lost in stars' embrace.

Galaxies spin in silent grace,
In the dark, they twirl and spin.
Mapping journeys we might trace,
To the depths where dreams begin.

Beneath this cosmic canopy,
Hearts unite in softest sighs.
We find our place in harmony,
As the universe replies.

In the quiet of the night,
Whispers carry hopes and fears.
Each twinkle a guiding light,
Illuminating all our years.

The Secret Symphony of the Night

Crickets sing their lullabies,
Filling air with soothing sounds.
Moonlight dances in the skies,
Casting magic on the grounds.

Every breeze a gentle note,
Rustling leaves in softest tune.
Stars above begin to float,
Underneath the silver moon.

Whispers weave a melody,
As shadows twirl in sweet delight.
Nature's vast tranquility,
Envelope us in the night.

In this symphony of dreams,
Harmonies of heart and soul.
Underneath celestial beams,
We discover we are whole.

So listen close to night's refrain,
Feel the rhythm, trust the beat.
In these moments, none in vain,
Life's true essence, pure and sweet.

Reflections in a Silver Stream

Ripples dance upon the water,
Mirroring the sky above.
Every wave a secret utter,
Carrying whispers of love.

Trees lean down to catch their sight,
Casting shadows, soft and warm.
In the glow of fading light,
Nature's peace remains the norm.

Each reflection tells a tale,
Of moments lost and found anew.
As the night begins to sail,
The stream unfolds its view.

With every glance, a story flows,
Time's embrace in quiet grace.
In this place, tranquility grows,
A mirror of nature's face.

Sit by the shore, let worries drift,
Allow the stillness to unfurl.
In the stream, find your gift,
As the world begins to swirl.

Tales of the Moonlit Glade

In the glade where shadows play,
The moon spills silver light.
Whispers travel, night's ballet,
Guiding whispers through the night.

Owls call softly from the trees,
As fireflies begin to bloom.
Every rustle in the breeze,
Brings the forest into swoon.

Stories hidden in the dark,
Waiting for a heart to hear.
Every creature leaves a mark,
Painting pictures crystal clear.

In this sacred, secret space,
Magic drapes the sleeping ground.
Underneath the gentle grace,
Nature's symphony resounds.

So tread lightly, listen close,
To the tales that nature weaves.
In this glade, we find the prose,
Of a world that never leaves.

Silent Whispers in Enchanted Corners

In the hush of twilight's glow,
Secrets dance where soft winds blow.
Petals sigh with gentle grace,
As moonlit dreams begin to trace.

Waves of silence weave the night,
Crickets chirp in pure delight.
Stars awaken from their sleep,
In corners where the fairies leap.

Softly flows the river's song,
Echoes linger, sweet and strong.
Whispers lilt through valleys wide,
In enchanted worlds, we glide.

Flickers of light weave through the trees,
As shadows dance upon the breeze.
Magic twirls in every glance,
Inviting hearts to join the dance.

Found in silence, secrets lie,
In these corners, dreams soar high.
With every breath, magic starts,
Silent whispers stir our hearts.

Shadowed Reveries of the Ethereal Path

Beneath the shroud of twilight's veil,
Whispers weave a ghostly tale.
Footsteps echo, softly tread,
In shadowed realms where dreams are bred.

Wandering through the misty night,
Stars awaken, twinkling bright.
Figures dance in moonlit haze,
As night unfolds its secret ways.

Silent echoes breath the past,
In shadowed dreams, our hearts will last.
Every turn a chance to see,
All the magic that could be.

Faintly brushing dreams of old,
Whispers of the brave and bold.
As shadows merge with twinkling stars,
We venture forth, forgetting scars.

Haunted trails beneath the sky,
Guide our spirits as we fly.
With each step, mysteries start,
Shadowed reveries touch the heart.

The Stillness of Mythical Footsteps

In the stillness, echoes lie,
Softly whispering a lullaby.
Footsteps whisper in the night,
Leading souls to realms of light.

Through the woods, a tale unfolds,
With each step, a magic molds.
Gentle breezes, secrets shared,
In the quiet, hearts are bared.

Cascading leaves in silent grace,
Embrace the dreams we dare to chase.
Every shadow tells a tale,
Of mythical paths where spirits sail.

In the arms of night's embrace,
We find our home, our sacred space.
With each heartbeat, time stands still,
In mythical realms, we bend our will.

Calling forth the magic near,
Listening closely, feel the cheer.
The stillness holds our wandering fate,
As mythical footsteps guide and wait.

Dreamscapes of Celestial Visions

In dreamscapes vast, we take our flight,
Guided by stars, twinkling bright.
Celestial visions weave the night,
In whispers soft, we seek the light.

Floating on clouds of gentle grace,
Time stands still in this sacred space.
Every thought a glowing spark,
Illuminating paths through dark.

Mountains rise in clouds of gold,
Ancient secrets to unfold.
In dreamscapes where the heart can soar,
We find the peace we've longed for.

Rivers shimmer with silvery sheen,
Reflecting all that's ever been.
In the stillness, futures gleam,
Crafted gently from a dream.

We wander through these painted skies,
Chasing hopes that never die.
Dreamscapes hold our gentle muse,
In celestial realms, we choose.

The Silence of Wandering Souls

In twilight's grip they drift along,
Their whispers soft, a ghostly song.
A winding path, lost in thought,
Eternal echoes, dreams forgot.

Through shadowed woods and silver streams,
They wander on with silent dreams.
Each step a tale, a sigh, a wail,
In the stillness where heartbeats pale.

Beneath the stars, they seek the way,
Through night's embrace till break of day.
A tapestry of hope and fear,
In solitude, their truths appear.

Across the fields where wildflowers grow,
They tread the earth with tales of woe.
Yet in their hearts, a glimmer glows,
Of love and peace that softly flows.

In gentle breaths, they find their peace,
As wandering souls, they seek release.
Through silence deep, they start to mend,
The bonds of time, they transcend.

Fragments of Stardust in the Mist

In midnight's veil, they softly spark,
Tiny jewels in the endless dark.
They dance on winds, with whispers fine,
These fragments lost in space and time.

Through veils of haze, they weave their light,
A thousand dreams in the endless night.
Each flicker shines with ancient grace,
A reminder of our shared embrace.

The cosmic tale, a wondrous flight,
Of stardust drifting, lost from sight.
Yet still they glow, a guiding flame,
In fleeting breaths, we call their name.

With every dawn, they fade away,
Yet in our hearts, they'll always stay.
A skyward glance, a wish we send,
For stardust dreams that never end.

In the soft sheen of a morning mist,
We find the jems that we once kissed.
Each fragment tells of stories past,
In memories, their light will last.

Chasing the Phantoms of Light

In the dance of shadows, they appear,
Phantoms flicker, drawing near.
Chasing beams that play and glide,
They vanish swift, like the tide.

A shimmering trail, a fleeting glance,
Illusions formed in twilight's dance.
Yet we pursue those glowing streams,
Lost in the echo of our dreams.

With every turn, they tease and taunt,
Elusive shades, we yearn to haunt.
In every ray, a chance to find,
The whispers of the light entwined.

Through fleeting moments, we chase the dawn,
In every shimmer, a story drawn.
But time escapes, like grains of sand,
Phantoms dance, just out of hand.

Yet in our hearts, they leave a spark,
A gentle glow in the deep dark.
Though they may fade and slip from sight,
We chase forever the phantoms of light.

The Heartbeat of Enchanted Moments

In fleeting glances, magic stirs,
Each heartbeat whispers, love's soft purrs.
A world aglow with colors bright,
In enchanted moments, pure delight.

Beneath the trees where secrets grow,
The silent winds begin to flow.
They carry tales of dreams anew,
In every breeze, a love so true.

With every laugh, a story spins,
A melody where wonder begins.
We hold our breath, just savoring,
The dance of life, the joy it brings.

In captured time, the memories weave,
Like golden threads in hearts we believe.
These treasured beats, forever gleam,
In the fabric of our sweetest dream.

As twilight falls, and shadows creep,
We cherish moments, forever keep.
With each heartbeat, a love that's pure,
In enchanted tales, we find our cure.

Shadowed Dreams in Pastel Hues

In twilight's soft embrace they lie,
Colors whisper as shadows sigh.
Gentle hues of faded light,
Carrying dreams into the night.

Misty thoughts like clouds will weave,
A tapestry of hopes we conceive.
Pastel skies tell tales untold,
Of moments cherished, brave and bold.

A brush of pink, a stroke of blue,
Memories dance in soft-filtered view.
Each color blooms, a soft caress,
Transforming pain to tenderness.

The stars, they glimmer, secrets share,
In dreams where shadows drift through air.
A quiet pull, the softest hue,
Pulls us deeper, a world anew.

In whispers of the evening's glow,
Pastel dreams begin to flow.
They carry us through realms of bliss,
A haunting peace in every kiss.

The Dance of Starlit Fables

Under a canopy of sparkling night,
Whispers of magic take to flight.
Stories born from twinkling eyes,
In the silence, the spirit flies.

The moonlight casts enchanting spells,
As every heart in wonder dwells.
Fables woven with silver thread,
In the dreams where silence spreads.

Celestial rhythms guide each sway,
Stars twinkle in a cosmic ballet.
Each flicker holds a timeless tale,
Of love and loss in a starlit gale.

With every pulse, the galaxies hum,
Echoes of where our souls come from.
Dance with shadows, embrace the night,
For in darkness, we find our light.

The universe cradles every sigh,
As we laugh, as we dream, as we fly.
In the starlit waltz, we dare to roam,
Fables echo, leading us home.

Secrets of the Ethereal Horizon

Beyond the edge of sight, we gaze,
Into horizons wrapped in haze.
Secret murmurs float on air,
Whispers of wonders, elusive and rare.

Golden light breaks the tender dawn,
A promise as the night is withdrawn.
The horizon glimmers, a distant call,
Inviting souls to rise, to fall.

Veils of mist cloak ancient lands,
Secrets slip through unseen hands.
With every breath, the world unfolds,
In shadows, the truth gently holds.

The sun kisses the edge of dreams,
Where reality blurs at the seams.
In the distance, echoes of flight,
Guide us softly into light.

The horizon stretches, wide and free,
Harboring the key to what could be.
With secrets shared beneath the skies,
We find our journey never dies.

Silenced Voices in Forgotten Woods

In shadows thick, the woods stand still,
Echoing whispers, a soft thrill.
Voices of yore, lost in the trees,
Carried away by the mournful breeze.

Branching tales weave through the air,
Secrets linger, silence lays bare.
Footsteps of time, soft and slow,
Trace the paths of those we know.

Lost echoes of laughter and tears,
Haunted by the weight of years.
Each rustle tells of a story passed,
In the embrace of the woodland vast.

A breeze sings softly through the leaves,
Telling of hearts that once believed.
In every shadow, a spark remains,
Of love and loss, of joy and pains.

Within these woods, the silence holds,
The beauty of life, the myths it molds.
In forgotten corners, voices sing,
Of moments that time cannot bring.

The Sound of Unseen Rain

Whispers fall from clouded skies,
Soft as dreams, where silence lies.
Gentle taps on windowpanes,
Nature sings her soft refrains.

Puddles form on cobblestone,
Reflecting light, a world alone.
Each drop a note, a secret song,
In the hush, where hearts belong.

Trees sway lightly in the breeze,
Dancing to the rain's sweet tease.
The earth is soaked; it drinks anew,
Life awakens, fresh and true.

In every corner, colors bloom,
Emerald greens, dispelling gloom.
With every breath, the world exhales,
A symphony that never fails.

Close your eyes and breathe it in,
Feel the magic deep within.
The sound of rain, a lullaby,
In unseen whispers, dreams can fly.

The Lush Resilience of a Hidden Haven

In the heart of tangled vines,
A world untouched by time, it shines.
Petals glisten with morning dew,
A sanctuary, strong and true.

Roots entwine, a hidden dance,
In whispered shades, a secret chance.
Amidst the thorns, the roses grow,
A testament of strength in flow.

Sunlight filters through the leaves,
Casting warmth, the heart believes.
In shadowed corners, life will thrive,
A vibrant pulse, forever alive.

Every breeze, a gentle sigh,
Cradles dreams that never die.
In quiet nooks, the stories hum,
Of battles won, and those to come.

So here's to grace beneath the shade,
Where beauty flourishes, unafraid.
In nature's arms, we find our grace,
A hidden haven, a sacred place.

Slumbering Echoes in Enchantment's Lane

In twilight's hush, the whispers blend,
With echoes of the night, they send.
Through corridors of moonlit air,
A dreamer's path, so light and rare.

The stars alight in patterns old,
Tales of love and wishes told.
Each shimmer holds a distant sigh,
In slumbering echoes, hearts can fly.

A lantern flickers, warm and bright,
Guiding souls through endless night.
With every step, the magic flows,
In shadows where the secret glows.

Where dreams can linger, softly play,
And capture hopes that drift away.
In this realm, all fears are lain,
Beneath the stars on Enchantment's Lane.

In cradled whispers, find your way,
To twilight realms where dreams hold sway.
A symphony of night unfolds,
In slumbering echoes, stories told.

The Lull of Stars Above

In velvet skies, the silence hums,
Where distant starlight sweetly drums.
A cosmic dance of light and dream,
The universe, a gentle stream.

Each twinkle speaks in tender tones,
Of ancient worlds and timeless bones.
In whispered lullabies, they weave,
A tapestry that hearts believe.

Beneath this dome, our worries fade,
The night's embrace, a soft cascade.
In that calm, our spirits soar,
The lull of stars forevermore.

As we gaze upon their glow,
Our thoughts take flight, our hearts bestow.
A quiet peace, we yearn to find,
In cosmic stillness, unconfined.

So rest beneath the starry sigh,
Allow the dreams to multiply.
In celestial arms, we trust,
The lull of stars, our hearts adjust.

Murmurs of the Enchanted Meadow

In the hush of twilight's glow,
Whispers ride the gentle breeze,
Petals dance in colors bright,
In this land where dreams find ease.

Beneath the trees, shadows play,
Secrets told in rustling leaves,
Delicate fragrances drift near,
Magic lingers, heart believes.

Streamlets twinkle like the stars,
Carving paths through emerald grass,
Nature's lullaby sings clear,
In this moment, time will pass.

Moonbeams weave a silver thread,
Across the meadow's quilted floor,
Where crickets serenade the night,
And fireflies dance, forevermore.

The breeze carries a sweet refrain,
Of hope and love, a soft embrace,
In this enchanted, sacred space,
The meadow sings, a timeless grace.

Reflections in a Moonlit Mirage

Beneath the moon's soft silver light,
A shimmering lake mirrors dreams,
Gentle waves in twilight's breath,
Carrying whispers, soft as beams.

Stars wink in the velvet sky,
Each one holding secrets deep,
Veils of mist glide gracefully,
Where silence lulled the world to sleep.

The night is a canvas of lore,
With shadows painted on the shore,
Time stands still, a fleeting pause,
In this realm where spirits soar.

Ripples break the tranquil scene,
As a cool breeze starts to sway,
Moonlit mirage tempts the soul,
To wander freely, lose the way.

Here, reality melts away,
Leaving traces of dreams anew,
In the heart of the night's embrace,
Reflections whisper, pure and true.

The Gentle Call of Celestial Creatures

In the depths of the cosmic night,
Softly calls the starry choir,
Voices of ancient memories,
Singing songs of dreams and fire.

Galaxies twirl in graceful dance,
Painting stories on heaven's face,
Each twinkle glimmers with romance,
A celestial love, a warm embrace.

Comets blaze with fleeting light,
Trail of glitter, paths of grace,
They whisper tales of distant worlds,
In the shadows of time and space.

The gentle hum of universe,
Rests on the heart of the night sky,
Inviting souls to drift and dream,
Where starlit wonders never die.

With every heartbeat, spirits rise,
To dance among the shining spheres,
The gentle call, an endless pull,
Celestial creatures, through the years.

A Symphony of Starlit Solitude

In the quiet of the evening,
As the dusk starts to unfold,
Stars awaken, one by one,
To weave tales both bright and bold.

The world below fades into shade,
While the cosmos begins to sing,
A symphony of solitude,
In harmony, the night takes wing.

Each note a shimmering embrace,
A serenade of cosmic grace,
In the stillness, hearts will pause,
To revel in this sacred space.

Moonlit paths invite the dreamers,
To wander where their hearts may lead,
Amongst the stars, in gentle whispers,
A peaceful mind, a quiet deed.

The universe hums softly on,
A melody, both sweet and deep,
A starlit solitude to hold,
In the night's embrace, we leap.

Voices of the Garden's Secret Keeper

In shadows deep, where whispers dwell,
The flowers converse, their secrets swell.
Guardian leaves, with tales to share,
Kiss the air with tender care.

Beneath the boughs, the silence sings,
Of cherished dreams and hidden things.
Roots intertwine in silent prayer,
Echoing hearts, a bond so rare.

The sun dips low, a golden hue,
Painting the world in shades anew.
Petals dance in morning's light,
Guarding stories of day and night.

Listen close, the breeze will speak,
Of love and loss, of strong and weak.
In every rustle, a promise rides,
As the garden blooms, the secret hides.

Eons pass, yet still they grow,
Guardians of what none shall know.
In their embrace, time stirs and weaves,
The essence of life, where magic breathes.

Reveries in a World Untouched

Where mountains touch the azure skies,
And rivers dance, a sweet surprise.
A realm untouched by human hand,
Where dreams take root upon the land.

Whispers of nature fill the air,
With melodies beyond compare.
Each leaf a note, each breeze a song,
In harmony, we all belong.

Beneath the stars, the night unfolds,
In mysteries, the universe holds.
Time stands still, as echoes sway,
Embracing night, embracing day.

The moon casts shadows, soft and pale,
Along the path of the unseen trail.
A journey through the wild unknown,
Reveries in whispers grown.

In this place of peace so rare,
A gentle heart will find its fair.
For in these dreams, we touch the sky,
And in our souls, the world will lie.

Breath of a Timeless Journey

Footsteps trace the path unworn,
In silence woven, destinies born.
Across the sands of time we roam,
In every heartbeat, we find home.

Waves echo tales of yore,
Carving edges on the shore.
Mountains rise and rivers flow,
Breathing life in ebb and glow.

Each moment's thread, a vibrant hue,
Stitching past and present too.
Horizons beckon, calling clear,
To venture forth, to persevere.

The sky ignites in colors bold,
As stars unveil their dreams of old.
In every dawn, a quest begins,
The breath of life, where hope begins.

Together we march, hand in hand,
Through valleys deep and sunlit land.
In the fabric of time, we believe,
That every journey helps us conceive.

Whims of the Arcane Lore

In twilight's grasp, where shadows play,
The ancient tales in whispers sway.
Mystic runes on parchment penned,
Awake at night, the secrets blend.

Beneath the moon, enchantments grow,
With whispers soft, the winds will blow.
Stars align; fate takes its flight,
In the realm of dreams, we take our sight.

Wanderers of the darkened glade,
Seek the magic that won't evade.
In every glimmer, in every sigh,
The essence of spells, they never die.

In hidden groves, the spirits dance,
Entwined in fate, a timeless trance.
Through misty veils, the truth reveals,
The arcane lore that twilight steals.

A tapestry in shadows spun,
Of worlds unseen, of battles won.
Embrace the wonders that life implores,
For the heart knows well the arcane's shores.

Gossamer Trails Through Mystic Woods

In shadows deep where silence dwells,
Gossamer trails weave magic spells.
Whispers of ancient trees align,
Secrets held in every vine.

Moonlight filters, soft and bright,
Guiding souls through realms of night.
Footsteps dance on dewy grass,
Time stands still as moments pass.

Echoes flutter on the breeze,
Carried from the heart of trees.
Crickets sing their nightly tune,
Beneath the watchful silver moon.

In twilight's grasp, the whispers grow,
Tales of old, in shadows flow.
Each step echoes stories told,
In the woods, both wild and bold.

With gossamer threads, dreams entwine,
Mystic woods, forever shine.
Nature's heartbeats, soft and low,
In this realm, the spirits glow.

The Sigh of a Twilight Breeze

The sun dips low, a fiery crest,
A twilight breeze brings gentle rest.
Soft shadows play on grassy knolls,
As night descends, embracing souls.

A breath of whispers fills the air,
Secrets linger, everywhere.
Golden hues fade to muted gray,
Time slips quietly away.

Crickets chirp a lullaby,
Underneath the vast, dark sky.
Stars awaken, one by one,
Guiding hearts until the dawn.

With every sigh, the world transforms,
Nature hums through shifting forms.
In twilight's heart, dreams interlace,
Where shadows hold a warm embrace.

Each breeze carries a fleeting thought,
Of moments lost, and battles fought.
In this magic, souls find ease,
In the sigh of a twilight breeze.

Starlit Murmurs Beneath the Canopy

Beneath the leaves, a world unfolds,
Starlit murmurs in whispers told.
The night awakens, soft and clear,
Calling out to those who hear.

Flickering lights in velvet skies,
Shimmering like forgotten sighs.
Echoes dance in moonlit streams,
Carrying softly, unspoken dreams.

Each branch sways with gentle grace,
Nature's rhythms find their place.
Dreamers linger, hearts exposed,
In this realm, where magic glows.

Woven tales of love and loss,
In starlit whispers, paths across.
Time is still, as night prevails,
In the hushed and sacred trails.

With every breath, the cosmos shares,
A universe of hopes and cares.
Beneath the canopy stretched wide,
Starlit murmurs, where dreams abide.

Whispers of the Forgotten Grove

In hidden corners, shadows play,
Whispers linger, fade away.
In the grove where silence reigns,
Echoes carry hopes and pains.

Ancient trees with twisted roots,
Hold the stories of old suits.
Fragrant blooms scent the air,
With secrets woven everywhere.

Time stands still, a breath held tight,
Each moment, a flickering light.
Memories dance on gentle winds,
In the grove where life begins.

With every sigh, a tale unfolds,
A tapestry of hearts and souls.
The past lingers, bittersweet,
In whispers soft, where shadows meet.

In the forgotten grove we roam,
Finding solace, making home.
Through every whisper, softly sown,
In nature's heart, we are not alone.

Resounding Dreams of Mythic Creatures

In twilight's glow, they dance and play,
Between the stars, they find their way.
With wings of silver and hearts so bold,
Their stories linger, forever told.

From mountains high to oceans deep,
In hidden realms, their magic sleeps.
With each bright flame of fleeting light,
They guide our dreams into the night.

Unicorns prance in fields of gold,
While phoenixes rise, their tales unfold.
In every whisper of the breeze,
Their echoes call, and souls appease.

So on we wander through the night,
With visions bright, and spirits light.
For in the dusk, they come alive,
And in our hearts, their dreams survive.

Together we chase those fabled sights,
In realms of magic, our hearts ignites.
In resounding dreams, we'll ever roam,
With creatures bold, we find our home.

The Solitude of Lost Pathways

Beneath the trees where shadows breeze,
Old pathways hide, longing to please.
With silence thick and whispers low,
A story lost, yet still aglow.

Every turn can shift the light,
Illuminating paths of night.
The past, a ghost that walks beside,
In solitude, we learn to bide.

Leaves rustle like forgotten tales,
On empty paths where silence dwells.
Each step is steeped in time's embrace,
A journey faint, yet full of grace.

The heart it yearns for roads once found,
In quiet moments, truth resounds.
Lost pathways tell of love and loss,
In every step, we bear the cost.

Yet in the still, a peace we seek,
Among the whispers, soft and meek.
These roads may fade, but still remain,
A solace born from quiet pain.

Enigmatic Shadows at Dusk

In fading light, the shadows creep,
Enigmas dance on secrets deep.
They swirl and twine around the trees,
A mystic hush, a whispered breeze.

Beneath the stars, they weave and sway,
In twilight's grip, they find their play.
With eyes that gleam and smiles that fade,
They tantalize the dreams we've made.

As night unfolds its velvet shroud,
Mysteries gather, eerily proud.
In every corner, lurking still,
The shadows beckon, hearts to thrill.

A fleeting glimpse, a chilling thrill,
In silence wrapped, we feel the chill.
Yet through the dark, we wander free,
With shadows casting dreams we see.

Enigmatic forms that shape our night,
In the fading glow, they take their flight.
With every heartbeat, truth will bloom,
In the dark's embrace, we find our room.

The Soft Resonation of Timeless Whispers

In gentle sighs, like morning dew,
The whispers float, a breeze so true.
With every breath, a tale unfolds,
In softened tones, the heart beholds.

Like echoes of the past they sing,
Timeless notes that memories bring.
A lullaby of fleeting grace,
In every sound, we find our place.

As twilight calls, the night awakes,
Each whisper dances, softly breaks.
Through moonlit skies and twinkling stars,
Their stories flow, no bounds, no bars.

In moments still, we pause and hear,
The timeless voice that draws us near.
With patience learned, we seek the sound,
In quietude, our souls are found.

So let us cherish every word,
In soft resonation, hearts are stirred.
For whispers grand, both near and far,
Guide us through, like a shining star.

A Veil of Mist and Starlight

In the whisper of night, shadows dance,
Moonlight weaves dreams in a gentle trance.
Echoes of secrets, softly confined,
Wrapped in the stillness, solace we find.

Stars shower glimmers upon the dark sea,
A tapestry woven, the night's mystery.
Veils of the cosmos, shimmer and twirl,
Embracing the night in a silken swirl.

Breath of the forest, tender and light,
Carried aloft on the wings of the night.
Mists weave their stories, old and profound,
Lost in the hush where the heartbeats sound.

Each twinkling light a wish yet to be,
Promises made in this ethereal spree.
Dance with the shadows, soft as a sigh,
In a veil of mist where dreams never die.

The Silence Between Heartbeats

In the quiet space where shadows dwell,
Echoes of whispers, secrets to tell.
Time holds its breath, a delicate pause,
Life in the stillness, a gentle applause.

Moments like petals, soft to the touch,
Fleeting and fragile, we cherish so much.
Lives intertwined in a heartbeat's embrace,
Finding the magic in time's quiet grace.

Breathe in the silence, hear the soft call,
In the depths of stillness, we rise, we fall.
Between every heartbeat, love sings its tune,
Guiding the lost like the light of the moon.

Journey within where the echoes reside,
Lost in the maze, where shadows collide.
In the silence, we find what we seek,
A pulse of existence, tender and meek.

Reverence of the Faery Glade

In a glade where secrets softly reside,
Whispers of magic, in shadows they hide.
Moonbeams caress the blades of the grass,
Time weaves enchantments that ever shall last.

Beneath the old oak, where faeries do play,
Glimmering laughter floats softly away.
Nectar of dreams drips from leaves overhead,
Cultivating wonder, where wishes are fed.

Moss cushions footsteps as soft as a sigh,
Winding paths beckon through twinkles of sky.
Sprites in the twilight dance under the stars,
They weave through the night like enchanting guitars.

Gathered around in the warm glow of light,
Spells and old stories enchant the deep night.
An offering whispered to woodland and breeze,
In the faery glade where our hearts find their ease.

Celestial Secrets Beneath the Canopy

Under the boughs of an ancient tree,
Stars dangle low in spirited glee.
Whispers of starlight, secrets unfold,
Carried by night with a shimmer of gold.

Leaves rustle gently, a lover's embrace,
In the dance of dusk, time slows in its pace.
Fingers reach up, connect with the skies,
Each twinkle a truth, a promise of highs.

Beneath this vast sky, dreams take their flight,
Cradled in shadows, embraced by the light.
Galaxies swirl in a cradle of night,
Holding our stories in infinite sight.

In the tranquil silence, the cosmos conspires,
To share with us hope, ignited by fires.
Secrets once hidden now flicker and gleam,
In the stillness of night, we awaken the dream.

Inked Whispers of a Wandering Soul

In shadows deep, the stories breathe,
Ink flows softly, tales beneath.
Wanderlust calls to a restless heart,
A journey begun, never to part.

Gentle winds carry secrets old,
Pages unfold with dreams untold.
Each new step, a canvas bare,
Inked whispers dance in the cool night air.

Under the moon's tender gaze,
The wandering soul begins to blaze.
Footprints linger like fleeting dreams,
Woven softly in starlit streams.

Through valleys and peaks, a tale unfolds,
In every heartbeat, truth molds.
Each whispered thought, a brand new start,
An inked melody flows through the heart.

As dawn approaches, colors collide,
A wandering soul no longer must hide.
With every brush of inked embrace,
The journey's essence fills the space.

Silent Strides in Forgotten Glades

In shadowed woods, where time stands still,
Silent strides echo, nature's thrill.
Among the trees, whispers awake,
A dance of stillness, the silence breaks.

Mossy paths twist in soft embrace,
Footfalls light in this sacred space.
Every leaf tells a tale of old,
In forgotten glades, secrets unfold.

Sunlight filters through branches wide,
A tapestry woven with nature's pride.
Streams murmur softness, breezes sigh,
In the heart of glades, dreams lie nigh.

Yet still, the silence holds its ground,
In rustling leaves, solace is found.
Each moment lingers, rich and deep,
Silent strides cradle the soul in sleep.

With every heartbeat, shadows blend,
Towards nature's arms, the weary tend.
In forgotten glades, life retreats,
Where silence and beauty gently meet.

Starlit Serenity in the Hushed Dusk

As daylight wanes, the dusk unfolds,
In starlit serenity, the world beholds.
Whispers of twilight embrace the sky,
In hushed tones, the day bids goodbye.

Stars pierce the veil of a darkened hue,
Each twinkle a wish, a promise anew.
The night serenades with its gentle hum,
In the stillness, the heartbeats become.

Through fields of dreams, shadows play,
In whispers of night, we drift away.
Moonlight bathes the earth in grace,
Starlit serenity finds its place.

The cosmos dances, a celestial reel,
With every glance, the spirit can heal.
In the hush of dusk, the world ignites,
As stars embrace the whispering nights.

Here in the quiet, freedom reigns,
Infinite wonders, no earthly chains.
Starlit serenity holds us tight,
In the heart of the calm, we take flight.

The Hushed Heartbeat of Night

In velvet dark, the night draws near,
A hushed heartbeat whispers, soft and clear.
Through the silence, a symphony flows,
Echoes of dreams where the soft wind blows.

Stars awaken with a gentle sigh,
Bathe the world in a celestial high.
Moonbeams dance with a tender light,
Embracing all in the hush of night.

Each breath we take, a secret shared,
With shadows weaving tales prepared.
The heartbeats echo in tender space,
In the soft embrace of the night's grace.

Night's quiet beauty wraps its arms,
In every whisper, lie hidden charms.
A serenade plays in the cool breeze,
The hushed heartbeat cradles with ease.

In dawn's embrace, the secret remains,
The night's heartbeat drives out the chains.
In every moment where silence clings,
The hushed heart whispers what the night brings.

Ethereal Footfalls in Midsummer's Night

In the glow of twilight's hue,
Footfalls soft, a quiet view.
Whispers stir the evening air,
Magic lingers everywhere.

Beneath the boughs, shadows play,
Fleeting dreams drift, fade away.
Stars emerge, a sparkling sight,
Guiding hearts through endless night.

In the distance, laughter sings,
Of gentle hopes that summer brings.
A dance of fireflies on high,
Lighting paths as they soar by.

Moonlit whispers formed in grace,
Stealing time in this sacred space.
Love's sweet embrace, softly spun,
In the night, two become one.

Each moment glows, a treasure rare,
Held in the warmth of lovers' care.
As echoes linger, dreams take flight,
Ethereal footfalls, pure delight.

The Gentle Sway of Time's Reflection

In rippling waters, secrets lay,
Time's reflection, night and day.
A gentle sway, a dance so fine,
Moments captured, so divine.

Leaves whisper tales of seasons past,
Memories held, a spell is cast.
Every heartbeat writes a line,
In the journal of design.

The sun dips low, the shadows blend,
Cycle of life, it twists, it bends.
Each tick, each tock, a fleeting grace,
Crafting stories in time's embrace.

Colors fade, but echoes stay,
Lessons learned along the way.
Nature's hands, both kind and cruel,
Teach us how to love and truly rule.

As twilight wraps the world in dreams,
We find our truth in silent themes.
Time, a river, flows on still,
An endless journey, a sacred will.

Whispers of Lore on the Winding Paths

On winding paths where shadows bend,
Footsteps trace where stories blend.
Whispers float on the evening breeze,
Carried forth through ancient trees.

Each bend reveals a tale so sweet,
Of lovers lost and battles beat.
Magic weaves through night and day,
Guiding hearts along the way.

Graffiti of the past unfolds,
In the twilight, a tale so bold.
Ghostly echoes in the air,
Speak of hope and deep despair.

With every step, the winds intone,
In every leaf, a world of stone.
Secrets waiting to be found,
In the silence, lost and bound.

The night unveils its tapestry,
A blend of fate and mystery.
All who wander feel the pull,
Of whispers soft and wonders full.

The Tranquil Echoes of Starlight's Dance

In the hush of night, stars gleam bright,
Painting dreams in silver light.
Each twinkle holds a story fair,
Echoes of love hang in the air.

Beneath the vast and endless sky,
Hearts unite, and spirits fly.
Galaxies swirl in cosmic tune,
Guiding souls by the light of the moon.

Soft whispers float on the breeze,
A serenade among the trees.
The tranquil seconds turn to hours,
As the world bathes in starlit showers.

In this embrace, all worries cease,
A moment held, a sacred peace.
Eyes closed tight, we drift and sway,
Lost in the dance till break of day.

The echoes fade yet linger near,
Each heartbeat felt, each shadow clear.
In starlit calm, we find our song,
In tranquil echoes, we belong.

Murmurs of a Hidden Realm

In shadows deep where whispers dwindle,
Secrets hide and dreams rekindle.
Ancient trees sway, their tales unfold,
A tapestry of magic, yet untold.

Beneath the moon's soft, silvery light,
Creatures dance in the quiet night.
They share their stories, lost in time,
In harmony, they weave their rhyme.

Crickets sing a lullaby sweet,
As starlight wraps around their feet.
Every crackle, every sigh,
A hidden realm where echoes lie.

The brook gurgles with laughter pure,
Its sparkling waters, a secret cure.
In these whispers, wonder grows,
A world alive where magic flows.

So listen close to the silent call,
Within the realm that enchants all.
For in the murmurs, truth is found,
In quiet corners, joy abounds.

Laughter of the Invisible Kind

In the corners where shadows leap,
A giggle stirs from the depths of sleep.
Unseen beings, full of cheer,
Their laughter dances, drawing near.

With every rustle, spirits play,
Invisible friends weave night and day.
In every breeze, a joyful sound,
A harmony of life unbound.

Through twilight's mist, the chuckles rise,
Moonbeams twinkle in twinkling eyes.
They twirl and spin in the autumn air,
With whispers soft, without a care.

In playful pranks, they find delight,
A world that glows with pure delight.
For laughter holds a timeless key,
To secret realms that all can see.

So let your heart embrace the play,
For joy exists in every way.
In laughter's glow, we come alive,
In invisible realms, we thrive.

Fantasy Beneath the Twilight Canopy

Underneath the twilight's cloak,
Dreams take flight as twilight spoke.
Stars awaken, shy and bold,
A canvas of stories waiting to unfold.

Fireflies dance in gentle sways,
Painting night with fleeting rays.
Each glimmer holds a fantasy bright,
A realm ignited by the night.

The trees listen to tales untold,
Whispering secrets both young and old.
Each branch sways, a secret share,
Of endless wonders lingered there.

A soft breeze stirs the evening air,
Carrying dreams beyond compare.
In whispers, the night calls us near,
To revel in hope, to conquer fear.

So let your spirit roam and soar,
In the twilight magic, find the core.
For every heart that dares to dream,
Will find the light, the hopeful beam.

Echoes Between the Emerald Leaves

In emerald groves where sunlight drips,
Echoes weave through nature's lips.
Each fluttering leaf, a story spins,
Of whispered secrets where life begins.

The rustling sound of branches sway,
Carries tales from faraway.
Listen close; you'll hear their plea,
Nature's heart, wild and free.

With every breeze, the echoes grow,
In harmony, they ebb and flow.
From roots to tips, the chorus sings,
A symphony of living things.

Between the trunks, the shadows play,
As sunlight filters through the gray.
In these moments, magic thrives,
In whispering woods, our spirit dives.

So wander deep, let silence guide,
Through emerald dreams, let your heart reside.
For in the leaves, the echoes breathe,
A timeless truth, we all believe.

Serene Nightfall in a Starlit Glade

The moonbeams dance on leaves so bright,
Whispering secrets in the night.
Cool breezes carry soft delight,
In this glade, all feels just right.

Crickets sing their soothing tune,
As stars awaken, one by one.
A tranquil world beneath the moon,
Where dreams and magic softly run.

Shadows play upon the ground,
Nature's heartbeats all around.
In this peace, our souls are found,
In starlit glades, we are unbound.

Every rustle tells a tale,
Of quiet nights and gentle trails.
Sorrow fades; we will not fail,
In the night's sweet, soothing veil.

As dawn awaits beyond the trees,
We linger still in softest ease.
With whispers of the night's cool breeze,
In this glade, our hearts find peace.

Echoes of Enchantment in Elysium

Glistening streams weave through the vale,
Carrying stories in their trail.
Emerald leaves in softest gale,
Echoes of magic, sweet and frail.

Flowers bloom with colors grand,
Calling us to this enchanted land.
In every touch, a gentle hand,
Whispers of dreams and hopes so planned.

Above, the skies in shades of gold,
Hold secrets yet to be retold.
In every heartbeat, tales unfold,
In vibrant life, we find the bold.

With laughter ringing through the air,
We find ourselves without a care.
In Elysium, joy we share,
A place where weary hearts repair.

Beneath the boughs, we take our stand,
With spirits free, we hand in hand.
In echoes of magic, we expand,
In Elysium's warm, embracing land.

Twilight Lullabies of the Celestial Realm

As twilight deepens, dreams arise,
In whispers soft beneath the skies.
The stars emerge with gentle sighs,
A lullaby that sweetly flies.

Colors blend in dusky hues,
As night descends and fades the blues.
In every note, a heart renews,
In melodies that love imbues.

Clouds like pillows softly drift,
Cradling wishes, giving lift.
In celestial arms, we find our gift,
A soothing peace, our spirits shift.

Moonlight bathes the world in grace,
Each shadow forms a tender space.
Through twilight's dance, we find our place,
In the celestial realm's embrace.

As nightingale begins to sing,
We welcome in the joy they bring.
In twilight lullabies, hearts take wing,
In sleep's sweet hold, forever cling.

A Serenade Beneath the Ethereal Sky

Underneath the vast expanse,
We find our place, we find our chance.
The night unfolds with a soft glance,
In whispers sweet, our hearts will dance.

Stars align in perfect rows,
As gentle winds caress our prose.
In this moment, beauty glows,
And in our dreams, the magic flows.

Clouds drift softly, fleeting light,
Guiding us through the peaceful night.
With every heartbeat, pure delight,
We lose ourselves in sheer twilight.

The heavens hum their tranquil song,
In harmony, we all belong.
With every breath, we join along,
In the serenade where dreams are strong.

As morning nears, the colors blend,
With hope and love, we start to mend.
Beneath this sky, we have no end,
In ethereal nights, our souls transcend.

Hushed Secrets Beneath the Boughs

Whispers flutter through the leaves,
Where shadows dance and time deceives.
Underneath the emerald dome,
Ancient tales find their home.

Moonlit paths that weave and twine,
Softly trace the roots of pine.
In the hush, a secret sighs,
Cradled where the stillness lies.

Fingers brush the mossy ground,
Listen close, the dreams abound.
In the quiet, memories swell,
Beneath the boughs, they weave their spell.

Stars above like lanterns glow,
Guiding hearts to places slow.
Each breath shared among the trees,
Sings of truths that float on breeze.

As day fades into gentle night,
Worlds unfold in silver light.
Here where spirits softly roam,
Hushed secrets find their way back home.

The Quiet Pulse of a Dreamer's Land

In the twilight, whispers thread,
Where the dreams of slumber spread.
Softly glows the hidden stream,
Reflecting every wayward dream.

Mountains rise like silent guards,
Holding stories, ancient shards.
In the valley, shadows play,
Crafting night from shades of gray.

Every rustle, each faint sound,
Echoes where, lost thoughts are found.
In the pause, the heartbeats sigh,
Mapping paths where dreams can fly.

Stars above, like watchful eyes,
Adorn the night's expansive skies.
Here in calm, the soul can see,
The quiet pulse of reverie.

As the dawn lends light anew,
Dreamer's land unfolds in view.
In the linger of night's embrace,
Life awakens with gentle grace.

Dreams Adrift in Shadowed Weald

Beneath the canopies so wide,
Dreams adrift in night abide.
Twilight's breath on emerald grass,
Holds the moments as they pass.

In the silence, echoes cling,
With the songs that shadows sing.
Footfalls soft on woodland floor,
Whisper secrets evermore.

Misty tendrils weave and curl,
In the night, the dreams unfurl.
Each one cradled, gently spun,
In the light of the waning sun.

Stars awaken, shy and fine,
Glimmering like aged wine.
Through the dusk, an unseen hand,
Guides the heart in shadowed land.

When the dawn begins to rise,
Glimmers dance in waking eyes.
Dreams, unbound, take their leap,
Crossing over from the deep.

The Stillness of Fabled Stars

Above the world, the stars align,
Fables woven, bright and fine.
In their stillness, stories gleam,
Whispering the night's soft dream.

Galaxies spin like tales untold,
In the dark, their magic's bold.
Each twinkle, a life once bright,
Carving paths in endless night.

Comets streak with fleeting grace,
Leaving traces in their pace.
In the hush, the cosmos breathes,
Crafting patterns in the leaves.

Through the silence, hearts can soar,
Finding wonders evermore.
In the night, an open door,
Invites the soul to explore.

When the dawn begins to sing,
Fabled stars take to their wing.
In the light, their tales remain,
Stored within the heart's refrain.

www.ingramcontent.com/pod-product-compliance
Ingram Content Group UK Ltd.
Pitfield, Milton Keynes, MK11 3LW, UK
UKHW021652200125
4194UKWH00003B/82